PENGUIN MODERN POETS 3

D 70

D0756406

Penguin Modern Poets

3

GEORGE BARKER

MARTIN BELL

CHARLES CAUSLEY

Penguin Books

Penguin Books Ltd, Harmondsworth, Middlesex, England
Penguin Books Pty Ltd, Ringwood, Victoria, Australia

—

This selection first published 1962
Reprinted 1964

—

Copyright © Penguin Books Ltd, 1962

—

Made and printed in Great Britain
by C. Nicholls & Company Ltd
Set in Monotype Garamond

Cover design by Peter Barrett

Contents

ACKNOWLEDGEMENTS

The poems in this selection are taken from the following books, to whose publishers acknowledgement is made: *Collected Poems 1930–55* (1957) and *The View From a Blind Eye* (1962), by George Barker, published by Faber and Faber; *Union Street* (1957) and *Johnny Alleluia* (1961), by Charles Causley, published by Rupert Hart-Davis. Martin Bell would like to thank several editors who first printed or broadcast a number of poems published here in book form for the first time.

GEORGE BARKER

'O Who will speak from a Womb or a Cloud?'

Not less light shall the gold and the green lie
On the cyclonic curl and diamonded eye, than
Love lay yesterday on the breast like a beast.
Not less light shall God tread my maze of nerve
Than that great dread of tomorrow drove over
My maze of days. Nor less terrible that tread
Stomping upon your grave than I shall tread there.
Who is a god to haunt the tomb but Love?

Therefore I shall be there at morning and midnight,
Not with a straw in my hair and a tear as Ophelia
Floating along my sorrow, but I shall come with
The cabala of things, the cipher of nature, so that
With the mere flounce of a bird's feather crest
I shall speak to you where you sit in all trees,
Where you conspire with all things that are dead.
Who is so far that Love cannot speak to him?

So that no corner can hide you, no autumn of leaves
So deeply close over you that I shall not find you,
To stretch down my hand and sting you with life
Like poison that resurrects. O remember
How once the Lyrae dazzled and how the Novembers
Smoked, so that blood burned, flashed its mica,
And that was life. Now if I dip my hand in your grave
Shall I find it bloody with autumn and bright with stars?
Who is to answer if you will not answer me?

But you are the not yet dead, so cannot answer.
Hung by a hair's breadth to the breath of a lung,
Nothing you know of the hole over which you hang
But that it's dark and deep as tomorrow midnight.

I ask, but you cannot answer except with words
Which show me the mere interior of your fear,
The reverse face of the world. But this,
This is not death, the standing on the head
So that a sky is seen. O who
Who but the not yet born can tell me of my bourne?

Lie you there, lie you there, my never, never,
Never to be delivered daughter, so wise in ways
Where you perch like a bird beyond the horizon,
Seeing but not being seen, above our being?
Then tell me, shall the meeting ever be,
When the corpse dives back through the womb
To clasp his child before it ever was?
Who but the dead can kiss the not yet born?

Sad is space between a start and a finish,
Like the rough roads of stars, fiery and mad.
I go between birth and the urn, a bright ash
Soon blazed to blank, like a fire-ball. But
Nothing I bring from the before, no message,
No clue, no key, no answer. I hear no echo,
Only the sheep's blood dripping from the gun,
The serpent's tear like fire along the branch.
O who will speak from a womb or a cloud?

Holy Poem IV

I

I am Saint John on Patmos of my heart
Towered and tabernacled with illusion;
Black Michaels and gold Satans stand at hand
Gulling me with their gestures of temptation
To bring me down from the marvellous mountains
Where in Babylonian gardens I find
Spinoza's face hanging from every tree
Murmuring love of all our kith and kind:
Or I feel, cold as a draught on my arm,
The spiralling universe like a worm
Coiling for comfort; and in my mind
The three-winged dove among my dreams
Moaning for its apocalyptic home.

II

I bleed Sebastian's brother on the ground,
No good it does me: or I hang my hand
My harp-hand on the Haman tree, but no –
My blood smiles from the ground in pride,
My hand makes music when winds blow.
There is no martyrdom worse than a life,
Nor can it be bought off with a sacrifice.
I cannot cut my body to Saint Peter's key,
Or, nipping off the hip-rose with a knife
Make me archangel, not with a kiss
Claim thirty shillings, for no one will buy
The plaster Jesus that my master is,
Crossed on my pain and crucified in my eye.

III

The monarch who wears a shrieking crown
Is us. All whipping tongues and words
Flash at our head and doom us down:
The sex of our cherubim is swords.
When we step down out of our beds or doors
The burning bush springs up between our feet;
Our smile is bright with tiger, and the days
Turn us like dogs in their drums. Then comes
Spinning and shining among us like wheels,
Throwing off visions to lead us home,
God – snatches me up in finger and thumb,
Douses me like a glimmer. And I see
Cruel to be kind to all his kind is he.

Resolution of Dependence

We poets in our youth begin in gladness
But thereof come in the end despondency and madness.
> Wordsworth: Resolution and Independence.

I encountered the crowd returning from amusements,
The Bournemouth Pavilion, or the marvellous gardens,
The Palace of Solace, the Empyrean Cinema: and saw
William Wordsworth was once, tawdrily conspicuous,
Obviously emulating the old man of the mountain-moor,
Traipsing along on the outskirts of the noisy crowd.

Remarkable I reflected that after all it is him.
The layers of time falling continually on Grasmere
        Churchyard,
The accumulation of year and year like calendar,
The acute superstition that Wordsworth is after all dead,
Should have succeeded in keeping him quiet and cold.
I resent the resurrection when I feel the updraft of fear.

But approaching me with a watch in his hand, he said:
'I fear you are early; I expected a man; I see
That already your private rebellion has been quelled.
Where are the violent gestures of the individualist?
I observe the absence of the erratic, the strange;
Where is the tulip, the rose, or the bird in hand?'

I had the heart to relate the loss of my charms,
The paradise pets I kept in my pocket, the bird,
The tulip trumpet, the penis water pistol;
I had the heart to have mourned them, but no word.
'I have done little reading,' I murmured, 'I have
Most of the time been trying to find an equation.'

He glanced over my shoulder at the evening promenade.
The passing people, like Saint Vitus, averted their eyes:

I saw his eyes like a bent pin searching for eyes
  To grip and catch. 'It is a species,' he said,
'I feel I can hardly cope with – it is ghosts,
  Trailing, like snails, an excrement of blood.

'I have passed my hand like a postman's into them;
  The information I dropped in at once dropped out.'
'No,' I answered, 'they received your bouquet of
      daffodils,
  They speak of your feeling for Nature even now.'
  He glanced at his watch. I admired a face.
  The town clock chimed like a cat in a well.

'Since the private rebellion, the personal turn,
  Leads down to the river with the dead cat and dead dog,
  Since the single act of protest like a foggy film
  Looks like women bathing, the Irish Lakes, or Saint
      Vitus,
  Susceptible of innumerable interpretations,
  I can only advise a suicide or a resolution.'

'I can resolve,' I answered, 'if you can absolve.
  Relieve me of my absurd and abysmal past.'
'I cannot relieve or absolve – the only absolution
  Is final resolution to fix on the facts.
  I mean more and less than Birth and Death; I also mean
  The mechanical paraphernalia in between.

'Not you and not him, not me, but all of them.
  It is the conspiracy of five hundred million
  To keep alive and kick. This is the resolution,
  To keep us alive and kicking with strength or joy.
  The past's absolution is the present's resolution.
  The equation is the interdependence of parts.'

GEORGE BARKER

Three Memorial Sonnets

(For two young seamen lost overboard in a storm in Mid-
Pacific, January 1940)

I

The seagull, spreadeagled, splayed on the wind,
Span backwards shrieking, belly facing upward,
Fled backward with a gimlet in its heart
To see the two youths swimming hand in hand
Through green eternity. O swept overboard
Not could the thirty-foot jaws them part,
Or the flouncing skirts that swept them over
Separate what death pronounced was love.

I saw them, the hand flapping like a flag,
And another like a dolphin with a child
Supporting him. Was I the shape of Jesus
When to me hopeward their eyeballs swivelled,
Saw I was standing in the stance of vague
Horror; paralysed with mere pity's peace?

II

From thorax of storms the voices of verbs
Shall call to me without sound, like the silence
Round which cyclones rage, to nurse my nerve
And hang my heart midway, where the balance
Meets. I taste sea swilling in my bowels
As I sit shivering in the swing of waves
Like a face in a bubble. As the hull heaves
I and my ghost tread water over hell.

The greedy bitch with sailors in her guts
Green as a dream and formidable as God,

Spitting at stars, gnawing at shores, mad randy,
Riots with us on her abdomen and puts
Eternity in our cabins, pitches our pod
To the mouth of the death for which no one is ready.

III

At midday they looked up and saw their death
Standing up overhead as loud as thunder
As white as angels and as broad as God:
Then, then the shock, the last gasp of breath
As grazing the bulwark they swept over and under,
All the green arms around them that load
Their eyes their ears their stomachs with eternals,
Whirled away in a white pool to the stern.

But the most possible of all miracles
Is that the useless tear that did not fall
From the corner of their eyes, was the prize,
The flowers, the gifts, the crystal sepulchre,
The funeral contribution and memorial,
The perfect and nonexistent obsequies.

To my Mother

Most near, most dear, most loved and most far,
Under the window where I often found her
Sitting as huge as Asia, seismic with laughter,
Gin and chicken helpless in her Irish hand,
Irresistible as Rabelais, but most tender for
The lame dogs and hurt birds that surround her —
She is a procession no one can follow after
But be like a little dog following a brass band.

She will not glance up at the bomber, or
    condescend
To drop her gin and scuttle to a cellar,
But lean on the mahogany table like a mountain
Whom only faith can move, and so I send
O all my faith, and all my love to tell her
That she will move from mourning into morning.

Summer Song I

I looked into my heart to write
    And found a desert there.
But when I looked again I heard
Howling and proud in every word
    The hyena despair.

Great summer sun, great summer sun,
    All loss burns in trophies;
And in the cold sheet of the sky
Lifelong the fishlipped lovers lie
    Kissing catastrophes.

O loving garden where I lay
    When under the breasted tree
My son stood up behind my eyes
And groaned: Remember that the price
    Is vinegar for me.

Great summer sun, great summer sun,
    Turn back to the designer:
I would not be the one to start
The breaking day and the breaking heart
    For all the grief in China.

My one, my one, my only love,
    Hide, hide your face in a leaf,
And let the hot tear falling burn
The stupid heart that will not learn
    The everywhere of grief.

Great summer sun, great summer sun,
    Turn back to the never-never

Cloud-cuckoo, happy, far-off land
Where all the love is true love, and
    True love goes on for ever.

Ode Against St Cecilia's Day

Rise, underground sleepers, rise from the grave
    Under a broken hearted sky
And hear the swansinging nightmares grieve
    For this deserted anniversary
Where, horned, a hope sobs in the wilderness
    By the thunderbolt of the day.

Footfall echoing down the long ruin of midnight
    Knock like a heart in a box
Through the aural house and the sibylline skull
    Where once Cecilia shook her singing veils,
Echo and mourn. Footstepping word, attend her
    Where, here, bird of answer, she prevails.

Sleep, wormeaten weepers. Silence is her altar.
    To the drum of the head, muffled
In a dark time, the sigh is a hecatomb.
    Tender Cecilia silence. Silence is tender
As never a voice was. Here, dumb-
Struck she mourns in the catacomb of her
      grandeur.

O stop the calling killer in the skull
    Like beasts we turn toward!
For was the nightriding siren beautiful
Caterwauling War until her bed was full
    Of the uxorious dead?
Let the great moaners of the seven seas
    Let only the seas mourn,
With the shipwrecked harp of creation on their
      knees
    Till Cecilia turns to a stone.

News of the World II

In the first year of the last disgrace
    Peace, turning her face away,
Coughing in laurelled fires, weeping,
    Drags out from her hatcheted heart
    The sunset axe of the day.

And leaning up against the red sky
    She mourns over evening cities:
The milky morning springs from her
        mothering breast
    Half choked with happy memories
    And fulfilment of miseries.

'I am the wife of the workman world
    With an apron full of children –
And happy, happy any hovel was
    With my helping hand under his gifted head
    And for my sleep his shoulder.

'I wish that the crestfallen stars would fall
    Out of his drunken eye and strike
My children cold. I wish the big sea
    Would pity them, and pity me,
    And smother us all alike.

'Bitter sun, bitter sun, put out your lions
    As I have put out my hope.
For he will take them in his clever hand
And teach them how to dismember love
    Just as though it was Europe.

'O washing-board Time, my hands are sore
   And the backs of the angels ache.
For the redhanded husband has abandoned me
To drag his coat in front of his pride,
   And I know my heart will break.'

In the first year of the last disgrace
   Peace, turning her face away,
Coughing in fire and laurels, weeping,
   Bared again her butchered heart
   To the sunrise axe of the day.

Turn on your side and bear the day to me

Turn on your side and bear the day to me
Beloved, sceptre-struck, immured
In the glass wall of sleep. Slowly
Uncloud the borealis of your eye
And show your iceberg secrets, your midnight
    prizes
To the green-eyed world and to me. Sin
Coils upward into thin air when you awaken
And again morning announces amnesty over
The serpent-kingdomed bed. Your mother
Watched with as dove an eye the unforgivable
    night
Sigh backward into innocence when you
Set a bright monument in her amorous sea.
Look down, Undine, on the trident that struck
Sons from the rock of vanity. Turn in the world
Sceptre-struck, spellbound, beloved,
Turn in the world and bear the day to me.

That Laddie's a Long Way from Home

That laddie's a long way from home, who loved
    Nothing the least
And everything most of all. He found
    The whole world best.

He went away to put his sweet arm around
    The star's waist,
And to give the glad eye to the Seven Sisters
    Who wink in the West.

When he whistled at the wide world she took him
    Close to her breast,
O that laddie's a long way from home, and long
    Long will he rest.

The Weepers in the Sacred Tree

Weeping, they spoke out of the sacred tree:
  'Dark and unloving powers
Envying everything valuable that is ours
  Determine human destiny.'

Smiling, they stroked the bird on my shoulder.
  'Bright bait,' they cried. 'Virtue!
Bringing down hammer and lightning upon the
    upholder.
  The dove shall desert you.'

Sighing, they showed anguish in their breast:
  'Look! Look!' they cried.
'The pain is eternal but the cause has died.
  Who cares what is best!'

Waiting for peace a victim at my foot
  Turned to stone with patience.
The voices murmured: 'Bitter the bitter fruit
  Of our supplications.'

Then out of the tongue-twisting tree spoke to me
  Every human and animal:
'We ask our parental cause why we had to be.
  Why do we live at all?'

'Why do the bright-eyed algae fold the shore
  Unloving in their embrace?
O unrewarded servants of Time and Place,
  Serve, serve no more.'

'Shuddering the great star uncurls at its sex
    In labour, but cannot give
  Back in the teeth of the universal multiplex
    A stellar negative.'

'O brute and hour, tooth and knife,
    Condemned to live and suffer and never die,
  Pronounce the unholy Why.
    Root out the assent at the source of life.'

  Subsiding the weeping ceased in the sacred tree
    As the leaves closed over
  And I saw the everlastingly restless body of
        humanity
    Clasped in the sins of its lover.

Channel Crossing

(To John Lehmann)

And just by crossing the short sea
To find the answer sitting there
Combing out its snaky hair
And with a smile regarding me
Because it knows only too well
That I shall never recognize
The axioms that I should prize
Or the lies that I should tell.

I saw the question in the sky
Ride like a gull to fool me, as
The squat boat butted at the seas
As grossly as through ultimates I
Churn up a frothy wake of verbs
Or stir a muddy residue
Looking for that answer who
Sanctifies where she perturbs.

The horror of the questionmark
I looked back and saw stand over
The white and open page of Dover
Huge as the horn of the scapegoat. Dark
It stood up in the English day
Interrogating Destiny
With the old lip of the sea:
'What can a dead nation say?'

As these words wailed in the air
I looked at Europe and I saw
The glittering instruments of war
Grow paler but not go from where

Like a Caesarian sunset on
The cold slab of the horizon
They lay foretelling for tomorrow
Another day of human sorrow.

But when I turned and looked into
The silent chambers of the sea
I saw the displaced fishes flee
From nowhere into nowhere through
Their continent of liberty.
O skipping porpoise of the tide
No longer shall the sailors ride
You cheering out to sea.

I thought of Britain in its cloud
Chained to the economic rocks
Dying behind me. I saw the flocks
Of great and grieving omens crowd
About the lion on the stone.
And I heard Milton's eagle mewing
Her desolation in the ruin
Of a great nation, alone.

That granite and gigantic sigh
Of the proud man beaten by
Those victories from which we die;
The gentle and defeated grief
Of the gale that groans among
Trees that are a day too strong
And, victorious by a leaf,
Show the winner he was wrong.

The continent of discontent
Rose up before me as I stood

Above the happy fish. Endued
With hotter and unhappier blood
Contented in my discontent,
I saw that every man's a soul
Caught in the glass wishing bowl:
To live at peace in discontent.

O somewhere in the seven leagues
That separate us from the stricken
Amphitheatre of the spirit,
O somewhere in that baleful sea
The answer of sad Europe lodges,
The clue that causes us to sicken
Because we cannot find and share it,
Or, finding, cannot see.

So in the sky the monstrous sun
Mocked like a punishment to be,
Extending, now, to you and me
The vision of what we have done:
And as the boat drew to the quay
I thought, by crossing the short water
I shall not find, in its place,
The answer with a silent face.

On a Friend's Escape from Drowning
off the Norfolk Coast

Came up that cold sea at Cromer like a running grave
   Beside him as he struck
Wildly towards the shore, but the blackcapped wave
   Crossed him and swung him back,
And he saw his son digging in the castled dirt that
      could save.
   Then the farewell rock
Rose a last time to his eyes. As he cried out
   A pawing gag of the sea
Smothered his cry and he sank in his own shout
   Like a dying airman. Then she
Deep near her son asleep on the hourglass sand
   Was awakened by whom
Save the Fate who knew that this was the wrong time:
   And opened her eyes
On the death of her son's begetter. Up she flies
   Into the hydra-headed
Grave as he closes his life upon her who for
   Life has so richly bedded him.
But she drove through his drowning like Orpheus and
      tore
   Back by the hair
Her escaping bridegroom. And on the sand their son
   Stood laughing where
He was almost an orphan. Then the three lay down
   On that cold sand,
Each holding the other by a living hand.

Cycle of Six Lyrics

I

The Dove of the Sea

O Doves, dismember me!
Here as I hang high
At my bone broken tree
Down from the bright fury
Descend with a wild cry.
O Doves, dismember me!

Spirit of those cold seas
That first were, and shall be
Last of the universe,
Alight, alight and be
Cold comforter to me.
O Love, remember us!

II

The Rose and the Rod

I saw the rose and the rod
Walk hand in hand on water
The bread of the creator:
Bulrushed our cradles rode
Wherever those two had trod
Generation burned on water.

O the rod, the rod is red
I hold in my hot hand,
And cold at the bedside
A ghost rose up and cried:
I rose from the grave's end
To prove no one has died.

III

Heroes and Worms

The dragons of the breast
Devour and drag down
Those seraphim of the mind
Who trumpet to attest
That Destiny is our own.
What is not is best.

I, cowboy with a spear,
Transfix my own heart
To kill the worm down there
Tearing St George apart –
But O that worm turns
Into my heart of hearts.

IV

Swansong of the Hyena

Where are those words that once
Alighted like swans upon
Our silent deserts of sense
And gave us oases?
They are all turned into stone
Like Memnon's effigies.

The rat and the hyena
Nest in my innermost
And sacred tabernacle.
I and my soul have seen
A vision of our foul ghost
And heard its mad crackle.

V

O Pearl and Breasted World

O pearl and breasted world
At whose green spring I slake
This bitterness of Ego,
And, a snivelling child,
Hush for its mother's sake,
Await my imago:

Let the natural causes
That unite us to
Our pearl and breasted mother
Exercise their forces
Till we are made to do
Justice by one another.

VI

Narcissus and the Star

I will not look within
Where at the hot pit hisses
A diet of worms and a demon
Adoring his mirror twin
More than any Narcissus
The issue of his semen.

But as the first and last
Dead suns rise and set
Over and hereafter
The sweet star and the past—
Glory without regret
For all things ever after.

The View from a Blind I

(Written at Hadrian's Villa)

From villa'd Tivoli
I look down over the plain
But like the view from a blind
Eye what I see is void.
Where once the Emperor
Mused in his alabaster
Court in a pool like a wheel
Saw he, perhaps, the same
Void in that psychic water?
Over the Campagna
As far as I can see
The farms flourish like flowers
And the confident olive
Whispers how civilized
Man and landscape can be.
Little rivers assure
The farmer of his reward
And a cynical Horace smiles
From a neat hillside that looks
Exactly like one of his odes.
O fountains of Tivoli
May crystal a single drop of
Your ostentatious torrents
Commemorate for one moment
– Flash in the sun and fade –
As bright a word as mine, then
On fostering laurel fall.
Over these gifted fields
The eye like a swift chases
Sporting among low eaves
Or skimming with lidded wings

An ariose Aniane.
As all these waterfalls
Render their copious
And votive offices
To this rivering valley
So, generous in their turn,
Seem all things here. Children
Bang and shout in the square
As ceaselessly as the fountains
Around them play. And high
Over it all the sun
Gazes like Hadrian.
And yet my blinded eye
Imposes upon the scene
A population of ruin,
The fallen pillar, the arch
Invested with poisonous ivy,
And from these vandalled tombs
Only the lizard like
A cicatrice shoots as I pass. Huge
As the sepulchre of a god
As degraded and as foregone,
Stranded in the wrong time
The Emperor's palace decays
Like ruins of the human spirit
Peopled with arthropods. So
Loud the Vox Populi
Echoes in these vast cells
As only valerian now
Rules where Hadrian reigned.
O how can the eye be so blind
As to look down upon those
Farms so fecund, so genial
With their windfalling gifts

Of what is at heart so wholly
Given to all that is good:
That true godsend, the source
Of generosity in man –
How can a neurotic I
Contemplate from its false
Altitude of self contempt
Such a prospect of truly
Holy Nature, and read
Its own faults into Eden?
Under the heavenly sun
The boys are simply at play.
Do fountains hesitate
To offer their perpetual
And charitable oblations?
The olive is liberal over
Her husbanding generations.
Not the broken Imperial pillar
With its gilt and faded laurel
Fallen, and only the snapdragon
Shuttling in its shade,
No, is not the last image and
Iconoclasm of our
Defiled and yet viable spirit.
The Roman Campagna
Covers with vines those bones
Whose great heart and soul
We have inherited,
As out of our living veins
And dying energies
Out of the shouting child
And our stony hearted I
The fountains of generation
Arise again and sing.

MARTIN BELL

The Enormous Comics
(A Teacher to his Old School)

Barnacled, in tattered pomp, go down
Still firing, battered admirals, still go down
With jutting jaw and tutting tooth and tongue,
Commanding order down cold corridors.

Superbly, O dyspeptic Hamlets,
Pause in the doorway, startle the Fourth Form
With rustlings of impatient inky cloaks –
Time and time again you go into your act.

Benevolent and shaven, county cricketers,
Heroes on fag-cards, lolling out of the frame,
Or smug and bun-faced, Happy Families,
Or swollen in shrill rage (Off With His Head!),

You lean huge areas into close-up
With cruel pampered lips like Edward G.
Robinson, or Tracy's anguished eyes,
And still remain the seediest of grandees.

Processioned hierarchically, larger than life,
Gigantic Guy Fawkes masks, great heads on
        stilts –
Your business was traditional, strictly articulated
Into timetables, only a few steps

From nightmare. Wild clowns will terrify
Wagging a wooden phallus at the crowd,
Raising a roar of response, of love and loathing –
Fat scapegoats stuck with broad rosettes of
        learning.

I listened and made myself little, still as a mouse
Watching the growling pussies at their antics –
Now I see, in the back row of any classroom,
Sharp impatient eyes, weighing me up for the
    drop.

Large masks creak. Sir will tear a passion to
    tatters.
One must pray for unobstructed moments,
For chances to be useful,
Like theirs, old wretches, like theirs.

A Benefit Night at the Opera

The chatter thins, lights dip, and dusty crimson
Curtains start dragging away. Then, at one bound,
A rush of trumpets, ringing brass and vermilion –
The frescoed nymphs sprawl in a sea of sound.

We give our best attention as we must, for
This music is fatal and must be heard.
The glittering fountains vocalize our lust,
The whole brilliant scene sways on to murder.

The idyll interrupted by a cough,
Coloratura soars into a fever.
After the vows, the sibyl shuffles off,
The conspirators' chorus mutter, melt away, leave us.

A traitor and his stabbed tyrant, downstage in tears.
Masked revellers are grouping for a wedding.
In stern beat start to life six scarlet halberdiers,
Move with the music, march to a beheading.

Lo! Wild applause proclaims a happy ending.
Vendetta is achieved with clinking swords.
Sheer from the battlements the Diva is descending,
Rash in black velvet and resplendent chords.

A Game of Royal Families

(From the French of Jean Pervert)

First of all the King. Where's the King of Hearts?
The King is in his counting-house, of course.
And what is he doing, is he counting
His money up, just as one would expect?
No, he's eating tarts, a great plateful
Of jam-tarts, blood-coloured jam-tarts
Stolen to frame the Knave of Hearts.
(He'll have to look to his muttons, that one.)
Then the Queen, what's she up to? Where but in
    her parlour?
But not with the Knave of Hearts, oh no!
The Queen's mouth is sticky with honey only
When the Jack of Clubs roughs her up.
No need to ask about His Grace
Of Diamonds and His Grace of Spades –
In the linen closet, as usual,
Enjoying unnatural relations with each other.
But where's the swaggerer, Knave of Hearts,
    where's he?
Where would you think, he's in the garden
With the maid.
But that's no alibi, that won't save his head.
They'll get at her through her father, the hump-
    backed joker,
And she'll tell some story about a bird from the
    sky
Pecking her nose off.
But what this lot don't reckon on –
The people think her baby something special –
When he grows up there'll be a revolution –
Hurrah! Hurrah! Hurrah! Hurrah! Hurrah!

Fiesta Mask

The raw feast rages in its fierce buffoons,
Flares in hot air. Calliope blares red.
Streamers, confetti, squeakers and fat balloons.
Here comes a great, big, daft, nid-nodding head –

A painted acre of face, a carnival grin,
With snouting nostrils, glistening carbuncles:
And children cringe, afraid to be sucked in
And eaten up by wickedest of uncles.

Once upon a time, some small boys found
In the next daylight's debris, after the revels
Had guttered down – the giant stretched on the
    ground,
Stupid in drunken sleep. The young devils

Began by throwing pebbles to sound the big head,
To find just what was under the disguise –
Started to claw the cardboard into shreds,
And one little bastard kept kicking at plaster eyes.

They battered at the craters he was breathing beer
    through,
Tore cheeks away in chunks. He didn't groan.
Soon there were ragged gaps enough to peer
    through.
And the squealing stopped. As if they'd been
    turned to stone.

A Prodigal Son for Volpone

Conspicuous consumption? Why, Volpone
Would splash it around as if he could afford it,
Wore himself out for his craft, a genuine phoney,
Who only wanted, gloatingly, to hoard it.

His son had sprung like a mushroom, pale in an
    alley.
Reluctant, they had to unload the stuff on him.
To cook the accounts, got Mosca back from the
    galleys –
These lawyers worried that the heir looked dim.

What was he, now, to do with all this gold?
His father had withered in prison because of it.
Root of all evil, he'd always been told
By scholars who'd brought him up. Get shot of the
    lot of it.

Gloomy vaults, cram-full roof-high with piles
Of metal and stone and paper shoved into sacks:
A great city's sewer, bustling golden miles
Swollen for carnival. Must give it back,

Somehow get rid of it, be a big spender.
The tradesmen knew of a new purse spilling around.
Not a junk-shop in Venice that wasn't stripped of
    its splendour,
Not a period-piece, not an objet d'art to be found.

How richly the *monde* assembled at his parties,
How thickly clustered in slow gilded whirls!
Sensitive business-men and butch aesthetic hearties,
Senile young statesmen, faint expensive girls.

'Spend it faster?' He'd pay on the nail for their
    answers.
A patron's deep-waving harvest was quick to be
    seen.
A sculptor in barbed-wire, a corps of Bulgarian
    dancers,
Three liberal reviews and a poetry magazine.

Mosca's smirk broadened. The Foundation showed
    a profit.
How white and stammering now our Volponetto!
'G-give it to the city. S-see the poor get some of it.'
He vanished aboard a waiting vaporetto.

For one odd halfpenny, Mosca broke on the rack.
The Senate's liver was hardened with golden wine.
Some money drained to the poor. The young man
    never came back.
Last heard of, was herding swine, or turned to
    swine.

Ode to Groucho

Invocation

Pindarick, a great gorblimey Ode
Soaring on buzzard wings, ornate,
Or tottering titanic on feet of clay,
It would have to be, to be adequate –
With the neo-gromboolian overtones
And the neo-classic gimmicks:
Pat gags cadenced from 'Mauberly'
In platinum-plated timing,
And tendrils convolvulating
To clutch the dirty cracks and hold the house up!

O flaking Palladian Palladium!
On a back-cloth rattled by oom-pah –
All our nostalgias, Hey there! the old vaudeville
    circuit.
Proscenium buttressed with brutal truths
Where sleek myths lean in manneristic attitudes,
Chalk-white in the chastest diction,
Sequined with glittering metaphysicality.
And massive ambiguities
Endlessly rocking a whole way of life.

Presence

What you had was a voice
To talk double-talk faster,
Twanging hypnotic
In an age of nagging voices –
And bold eyes to dart around
As you shambled supremely,
Muscular moth-eaten panther!

Black eyebrows, black cigar,
Black painted moustache –
A dark code of elegance
In an age of nagging moustaches –
To discomfit the coarse mayor,
Un-poise the suave headmaster,
Reduce all the old boys to muttering fury.

A hero for the young,
Blame if you wish the human situation –
Subversivest of con-men
In an age of ersatz heroes:
Be talkative and shabby and
Witty; bully the bourgeois;
Act the obvious phoney.

Apotheosis

Slickness imposed on a rough beast,
A slouching beast and hypochondriac.

Great Anarch! Totem of the lot,
All the shining rebels

(Prometheus, of course, and that old pauper
Refusing cake from Marie Antoinette,
And Baudelaire's fanatical toilette,
And Rimbaud, striding off to Africa,
And Auden, scowling at a cigarette . . .)

Bliss was it *etc*. Smartish but fair enough.
We stammered out our rudenesses

O splendid and disreputable father!

To Celebrate Eddie Cantor

The flesh is brittle, alas,
And ever-modish time, that fiend, is slee:
The Goldwyn Girls of Nineteen Thirty-Three
Also must go, must fade beyond nostalgia,
Vanish when celluloid crackles.

That year, not less constrained,
We strained the other way to find the future –
Eager and awkward, tried to look sixteen,
Be full initiates into the life of the time
And shuffle into the LYRIC, the local flea-pit.
We howled and whistled, fidgets on iron seats.

Our coming-in was brisk to music
Strident through raucous light along the slanting
        floor,
Underfoot rubbish and everywhere sweet
        disinfectant
Stinking like LADIES and GENTLEMEN –
The whole place blatant and blaring,
Usherettes sullen and louts obstreperous.

And, slumping back in seats, to see a flick,
Shadows to look at shadows, not expecting luck,
Amazed then, caught in your outrageous joy,
Dear Eddie!
                Blank looming screen
And then you whirled from its imagined wings –
A small impassioned man who could hardly wait
        for his music,
A master, from Vaudeville, an accomplished
        master.

Voice soaring in gleeful lubricity,
Scandalous coloratura at full tilt!
Excited wide eyes rolling
And hands that have to clap that joy's too much.
Energy, wanton small bright ball
Leaping on top of the fountain –
Living water, extravagant
Flooding and cleansing the movie-house.

No endless exits down the sad perspectives,
The avenues of infinite regrets,
For you, Sir, No Siree!
Palmy Days, ample a blue sky
And the gross bull lulled to an euphoric calm,
Contented cows, O Don Sebastian –
The lineaments of gratified desire.
Making whoopee with the whooping red-skins.

Thinly we rustled, ears of unripe corn –
You could have gathered us up in the palms of
    your hands.
Singing and dancing, you came out more than real,
Potent Revivalist, strong drink for shadows –
For you at the end of the picture
Bunches and baskets of flowers, all of them girls.

Ode to Himself

I

Go on, good monkey, make your bow, be me.
Appear as the polite one, the sensitive
Shy one, awkward but helpful,
Monkey of wisecracks, monkey who knows the
    words.

This social creature must ignore
All his disgraces, all the deplorable monkeys;
They antic behind his back as if they were at
    home:
Evil-tempered monkey with weak rage,
Envious idle incompetent monkey
A spiteful mimic of more handsome apes,
Belching wasteful monkey, timid
Monkey of tiny dishonesties.

Sad monkey, a self-pitying one,
Unlucky monkey, monkey who was framed
By mean streets in the shabby years –
Poor wretch of a monkey
In the freezing winds of time,
Almost a brass monkey.

Miniature snarling super-ego monkey
Squatting on the shoulder of the gross orang-
    outang

And stinking cynical monkey
Planning small satisfactions
In face of an abstract nothing –
What a nest of nasty negative monkeys!

II

Safer not postulate a central *me*
To be ambitious about all this
This chattering toyshopful of monkey puppets.
No puppet-master stoops
To curb their messy antics: monkey business
Must be endured
If only as talk in the head.

To watch is possible: therefore you must watch.
Sit down. Sit still. Eat your damned apple up.
The largest virtue is to pay attention,
Then watch intently, watcher in the dark –
Watch how a jangling piano-range of strings
Dangles a reigning Kong for every minute,
Wearing your shirt and tie, your beard, your
    spectacles,
Inflections of your voice and gestures of your
    hands,
Grimaces and grimaces and grimaces.

Old monkeys never die, fight back and never die.
They might fade away if you watch them.

And some already folding up their strings
Will lie down neatly in a cardboard box.
R.I.P. monkey. Then again, R.I.P. monkey.

New beasts keep crowding in the wings.
Here come the vulgarest clowns, red-cheeked
    baboons
With their pea-nuts and bananas.
Out-stare them. Staunchly watch.

III
The legends say the monkeys drift to sleep
Under clear scrutiny of evening sky,
Puff into cloud-shapes, fade away

And branches prick, impressive silhouette,
Pattern of monkey-puzzle tree.

Reason for Refusal

Busy old lady, charitable tray
Of social emblems: poppies, people's blood –
I must refuse, make you flush pink
Perplexed by abrupt No-thank-you.
Yearly I keep up this small priggishness,
Would wince worse if I wore one.
Make me feel better, fetch a white feather, do.

Everyone has list of dead in war,
Regrets most of them, e.g.

Uncle Cyril; small boy in lace and velvet
With pushing sisters muscling all around him,
And lofty brothers, whiskers and stiff collars;
The youngest was the one who copped it.
My mother showed him to me,
Neat letters high up on the cenotaph
That wedding-caked it up above the park,
And shadowed birds on Isaac Watts' white shoulders.

And father's friends, like Sandy Vincent;
Brushed sandy hair, moustache, and staring eyes.
Kitchener claimed him, but the Southern Railway
Held back my father, made him guilty.
I hated the khaki photograph,
It left a patch on the wallpaper after I took it down.

Others I knew stick in the mind,
And Tony Lister often –
Eyes like holes in foolscap, suffered from piles,
Day after day went sick with constipation
Until they told him he could drive a truck –

Blown up with Second Troop in Greece:
We sang all night once when we were on guard.

And Ken Gee, our lance-corporal, Christian
    Scientist –
Everyone liked him, knew that he was good –
Had leg and arm blown off, then died.

Not all were good. Gross Corporal Rowlandson
Fell in the canal, the corrupt Sweet-water,
And rolled there like a log, drunk and drowned.
And I've always been glad of the death of Dick
    Benjamin,
A foxy urgent dainty ball-room dancer –
Found a new role in military necessity
As R.S.M. He waltzed out on parade
To make himself hated. Really hated, not an act.
He was a proper little porcelain sergeant-major –
The earliest bomb made smithereens:
Coincidence only, several have assured me.

In the school hall was pretty glass
Where prissy light shone through St George –
The highest holiest manhood, he!
And underneath were slain Old Boys
In tasteful lettering on whited slab –
And, each November, Ferdy the Headmaster
Reared himself squat and rolled his eyeballs upward,
Rolled the whole roll-call off an oily tongue,
Remorselessly from A to Z.

Of all the squirmers, Roger Frampton's lips
Most elegantly curled, showed most disgust.
He was a pattern of accomplishments,

And joined the Party first, and left it first,
At OCTU won a prize belt, most improbable,
Was desert-killed in '40, much too soon.

His name should burn right through that monument.

No poppy, thank you.

Dreams of Evasion

I

Deeper and deeper into softer moss
Like rolling downs, but swamp, electric-green
Velvetest counterpane but deeper in

Reeds pricking, sinuous knitting-needles, bunched
Further and deeper in to buzzing confusion
Where flowers eat burnished insects

Tufted sods sink, bristle, go soft
Stamp if you like, tread something flat
Shod feet will cut sharp shapes, but now

Footprints are filling vaguely with
Seeping, spread to shapes of bruises
Sucking is always starting under your feet

II

Water haze dazzles, spits on face
Flickering adders, threads of streams
Stitch, stitch, a brilliance, nets of spiteful talk
Incessant glitter and chatter, theft of soil

Zips gripping, streams bite, bite their way
Urgent to the river. There it lolls
A glint, through greasy banks. And nudges
It has eaten its contours into smiling curves

III

Must get away, must not get wet or dirty
Always a way out, always a bridge
Round the next bend, before the silver sewage

Dimples to whirlpools, piles to a weir
Be clever, find the fussy steps to reach a
Safe structure strutting, riveted in air

A saving thought commits, betrays
To muscles bulging twisted, sickening strides
Struggle for balance on the shining slopes
Of banks of slime
Straining to hold a distance from yourself
Blur lurching up, self in a mirror of mud

IV

On to the multipurpose bridge
Ambitious architecture vast hotel
Delicate metal blue-print convolution
Closet catwalk ingle oubliette
Ballrooms glaring jaded chandeliers
(Somebody's got to swing)
Bookwalled dens lined charts of Yarmouth say
And footman, footman, footman phoning columns
Frequent in alcoves
Tip the Vice-Chancellor something handsome
And pump the Padre's palm before you're topped
Climb, crawl, clamber, stroll or stride tiptoe
Polished corridors to priestholes
Stammer up mile-wide winding marble stairs
To bedroom, bedroom, bedroom, royal bedroom
(A good chap in a suit will arrange everything)
Avoid gymnastic apparatus, sides of ships
And small back rooms with private guillotines
Up and down in the lift from unmade bed to
      unmade bed
Through honeycombed conveniences slithered
      with shit.

The ladder with the mathematic steps
(Ten seconds to solve each equation)
Leads to the gilt chairs of the Senate Chamber
Through a mouse-slit in the ceiling

One's scared to fall and does of course and
Screams right through the drop
                                        Falls
And hopes to wake up

Hypochondriac Reading Newspaper

The sun-lit surface shrugs. An easy day ...
No extra effort needed
To keep down monsters coiling underneath,
The hunched muscles writhing
In private hells, the gas-lit punishment cells.

Strained morning-face in the train
Keeps stoic lines, though careful to have ready
Accommodation, tolerant knowing eyes:
Only eager to relax, be safe a little,
Melt to a decent shape in smiles.

But always eyes find words to jerk fear back,
Something gross to be afraid of,
A thought to block the sun:
A twist in the dimensions
That can't be laughed away or worked away.

The ghosts are dwindled, only to re-form
More brassily efficient:
(Pale SYPHILIS deflated, pinked by penicillin –)
And see they all come back, infectious breaths,
Compulsive gripes to hold us gibbering

Bold CANCER, famous BOMB, blonde TELEVISION,
And statistical pressure of PUBLIC OPINION.

The Songs

Continuous, a medley of old pop numbers –
Our lives are like this. Three whistled bars
Are all it takes to catch us, defenceless
On a District Line platform, sullen to our jobs,
And the thing stays with us all day, still dapper,
    still Astaire,
Still fancy-free. We're dreaming while we work.

Be careful, keep afloat, the past is lapping your chin.
South Of The Border is sad boys in khaki
In 1939. And *J'attendrai* a transit camp,
Tents in the dirty sand. Don't go back to Sorrento.
Be brisk and face the day and set your feet
On the sunny side always, the sunny side of the
    street.

Winter Coming On

(A caricature from Laforgue)

Fine feelings under blockade! Cargoes just in
    from Kamschatka!
Rain falling and falling and night falling
And how the wind howls . . .
Halloween, Christmas, New Year's Day
Sodden in drizzle – all my tall chimneys –
Industrial smoke through the rain!

No sitting down, all the park-benches are wet.
It's finished, I tell you, till next season.
Park-benches wet and all the leaves rust-eaten,
Horns and their echoes – dying, dying . . .

Rally of rain-clouds! Procession from the
    Channel –
You certainly spoiled our last free Sunday.

Drizzles:
And in wet woods the spiders' webs
Weigh down with rain-drops: and that's their lot.
O golden delegates from harvest festivals,
Broad suns from cattle-shows,
Where have they buried you?
This evening a sun lies, shagged, on top of the
    hill,
On a tramp's mattress, rags in the gorse –
A sun as white as a blob of spittle
On tap-room saw-dust, on a litter of yellow gorse,
Of yellow October gorse.
And the horns echo and call to him –
Come back! Won't you come back?

View halloo, Tally-ho ... Gone away.
O oratorio chorus, when will you be done?
Carrying on like mad things ...
And there he lies, like a torn-out gland on a neck,
Shivering, with no one by.

Tally-ho, then, and get on with it.
It's good old Winter coming, we know that.
By-passes empty, turnings on main roads
With no Red Riding Hood to be picked up.
Ruts from the wheels of last month's traffic –
Quixotic tram-lines to the rescue of
Cloud-patrols scurrying
Bullied by winds to transatlantic sheep-folds.
Get a move on, it's the well-known season
        coming, now
And the wind last night, on top of its form,
Smashing suburban front-gardens – what a mess!
Disturbing my night's sleep with dreams of axes.

These branches, yesterday, had all their dead
        leaves –
Nothing but compost now, just lying about.
Dear leaves of various shapes and sizes
May a good breeze whirlpool you away
To lie on ponds, decorative,
To glow in the park-keeper's fire,
To stuff ambulance mattresses, comforts
For our soldiers overseas.

Time of year, time of year: the rust is eating,
The rust is gnawing long miles of ennui,
Telegraph-wires along main roads, deserted.

Horns, again horns ... the echoes dying,
Dying ...
Now changing key, going north
With the North Wind, Wagnerian,
Up to all those bloody skalds and Vikings ...

Myself, I can't change key; too many echoes!
What beastly weather! Good-bye autumn,
        good-bye ripeness ...
And here comes the rain with the diligence of an
    angel.
Good-bye harvest, good-bye baskets for nutting,
And Watteau picnics under the chestnut trees.
It's barrack-room coughing again,
The landlady's horrible herbal tea –
It's TB in the garden suburb,
All the sheer misery of satellite towns.

Wellingtons, long underwear, cash chemists,
        dreams,
Undrawn curtains over verandas, shores
Of the red-brick sea of roofs and chimney-pots,
Lamp-shades, tea and biscuits, all the picture
    papers –
You'll have to be my only loves!
(And known them, have you? ritual more portentous
Than the sad pianos tinkling through the dusk,
The registrar's returns of births and deaths,
In small type weekly in the press.)

No! It's the time of year, and this clown of a
    planet!
O please let the wind, let the high wind

Unknit the bed-socks Time is knitting herself!
Time of year, things tearing, time of year!
O let me every year, every year, just at this time
Join in the chorus, sound the right sour note.

Corbiere: The Ballad Singer at the Pardon of St Anne

I

Blessed the barren dunes,
Stark nude like the sea –
And the chapel of Anne-of-Palud
Is crude, too, and holy,

Of St Anne, the Good Gossip,
A granny for young Jesus
In rotting oak beneath a rich
Cope . . . richer than Croesus.

Beside her, the Virgin is small –
Fragile distaff, waiting for *Angelus* –
And St Joseph, upstaged, in his niche
Shoves his candle at us.

It's Her Pardon – fun and games and
Mystery – the stubble's hopping with fleas –
Anne, Sainted Ointment, cure-all
For mothers-in-law, and husband's ease.

From the parishes round about,
From Plougastel and Loc-Trudy,
They've arrived already, camping out
Three nights, three days, up till Monday.

Three days, three nights, the salt-marsh blares
With music – the rite's traditional –
Heavenly choir and singing drunks –
Beginneth the SACRED CANTICLE.

II

O Mother, carved out with a chopper
From oak heart, hard and good,
Your gold robe hides a solid Breton
Soul, all one piece, honest wood.

Green crone with a used-up face,
Boulder under the flood,
Fretted by tears of love,
Parched by tears of blood.

You, whose shrivelled breasts
Were plumped again, to carry
A purposeful virginity –
The Virgin Mary.

Proud housekeeper, mistress and servant,
Related to the Almighty,
The poor are pleased to talk to you
For you answer them politely.

A wand for the blind, and crutches
For cripples, arms for the new-born,
A mother for Madame your Daughter –
You've adopted all the forlorn.

Blossom of new maidenhead!
Fruit of wife's swollen udder!
Garden of rest for the widow!
District Nurse for the widower!

Joachim's Arch! O Ancestress!
Four-leaf clover! Mistletoe bough!
Medallion with a rubbed-out face!
Horeb! Jesse's Rod! Our way!

You kept the fire in
And went on with your knitting
As darkness came down round your lap
Where the Child was sitting.

You were there, the one who could cope,
Making garments in Bethlehem,
Still there, stitching the shroud,
Grief-stunned in Jerusalem.

Your face is a wrinkled map
Of crosses – your hair white as linen –
Keep from pedantic evil eyes
The cots of our grandchildren.

The born, the not-yet born,
Bring on, and keep them well,
And smuggle water from your tears
When God isn't looking, to Hell.

Take back little children
In white nightgowns, fading away,
And summon the old who are bored
To the everlasting Sunday.

O growl! The Virgin's Dragon!
Keep the crib safe and secure,
And keep bitching at Joseph
To sweep round the front door.

Pity the girl in the family way
And the small boy lost on the road –
If anyone throws a stone
Change it into bread.

Beacon on sea and on land,
Harbour, stars over heath,
Good Lady, through tempest, through war,
You beckon towards a good death.

Humble; no star at your feet –
Humble and strong to save –
Your veil in the clouds means peril,
Pale halo over the wave.

Those whose lives are a mess
– Begging pardon – sunk in the booze –
Show them the steeple and clock,
The road back to the house.

Fire the Christians hereabouts
With your own zeal, gentle and chaste,
And gather your simples, Wise Woman,
To soothe the horned beast.

Be an example to housewives
Of work and fecundity –
And say hullo to our relations
Already in eternity.

We'll line up an army of candles –
Spermaceti – the best – all the way
Round your chapel. We'll celebrate
Low mass at the break of day.

Keep our hearths safe
From spells and folk who are spiteful . . .
We'll give you at Easter
Flax, a whole distaff-full.

If our bodies stink on earth
Your grace is a bath for our good:
Shower on us in this graveyard
Your wholesome odour of sainthood.

Till next year, then. Here's your candle,
(Three half-crowns it's cost me).
Respects to Madame the Virgin,
Not forgetting the Holy Trinity.

III

And the faithful, in penitent nightshirts,
— *St Anne, have pity, please* —
Drag themselves round the church
Three times, on their knees.

And go on to drink the waters,
Miraculous now, from the hole
Where scabby Jobs have bathed . . .
Your faith has made you whole.

Down there they hold their suppers,
The wretched, Jesus's brethren,
And you won't see any miracles,
But real holes: *Put your finger in . . .*

On their hurdles they look like saints,
With scarlet nimbuses, each one
An owner of extensive sores
Like rubies glinting in the sun.

A barking man with rickets
Just can't stop his arm-stump's twitch —
Can't help elbowing the epileptic
Having a fit in the same ditch.

By a tree-trunk, mistletoe-bitten,
Stands a man with an ulcer that bites –
And a mother and daughter are dancing –
Choreography by St Vitus.

A father heats up a poultice
For a small son who's not thriving:
A boy owes a lot to his father –
The chancre earns their living.

There's an idiot since he was born,
An angel-blasted simpleton,
Ecstatic in his innocence –
The simple are close to heaven.

Watch, passer-by, all passes ... but
The idiot's stare is stone and firm –
He must be in a state of grace,
For grace is outside time.

Among the crowd after evensong,
When the holy water's sprayed us,
A corpse sticks out, alive, a long
Leper ... relic of the crusaders.

Then those who the kings of France
Used to cure with a touch –
Since France has cut off her kings,
Their God's cut his mercy by that much.

Put something into their bowls –
All our forefathers carried it,
The Fleur-de-Lys of King's Evil
Which these are chosen to inherit.

Miserere then for the junketings
Of these dirty old outcast Bretons ...
But stumps can be managed like pincers
And crutches are weapons.

Venture among them, able-bodied,
But take care to keep your fleece on –
Beware of fingers that hook, of legs
Fixed in *Kyrie Eleison*.

And if you'd be sight-seeing, dear,
Take a look and turn back quick –
From under these scraps of rags
A scrap of flesh might prick.

They're hunting on their own estates
With Arms emblazoned on their skins!
Their hands have the *droit de seigneur*
Over anything clutched therein.

Offerings heaped – of rotting meat –
Heaven's elect – with death-house features –
They make themselves at home with God
For surely they're his creatures.

They're swarming in the churchyard –
As if the dead mistook the Day
Of Judgement, crawling out from stones
That crush the limbs they drag away.

We've no right to talk – they're sacred.
It's Adam's sin they're punished for.
The Almighty's finger has marked them,
The Almighty's right be praised therefore!

The scapegoats of the bellowing flock,
Loaded with every sin we're at,
God works his anger off on them!
The vicar of St Anne's is fat.

IV

But a palpitating note,
A gasping echo in the breeze,
Cuts across the grumbling drone
Of this walking purgatory.

Keening like a beast in pain,
She stands beside the Calvary,
Half a blind beggar, as it were,
No dog and only one eye. –

A weather-bitten ballad-singer,
Drop a halfpenny in her hat
And she'll do you *Abaylar, Wandering Jew*,
Or any other old favourite.

O but her song is long-drawn-out,
Complaining like a thing ill-used,
Like a long day with nothing to eat,
So lamentable her blues.
She sings just as she breathes, a bird
Without a nest, with no fine feathers,
Battering blindly as she flies
Round granite God, in granite weather.

She can talk, too, if that matters,
As far as she can see she thinks –
The main road keeps stretching before her –
If she gets hold of sixpence, she drinks.

A woman, oh dear yes – her skirt
Is strings held together by string:
Black teeth grip an empty pipe –
Life is full of excellent things!

Her name? Call her Misery.
Got herself born, somehow, somewhere –
Somewhere, someday will be found dead –
There'll be no fuss, no one will care.

If you come across her, poet,
Humping her army kit-bag –
Please recognize our sister,
Give her a few fills of shag.

You'll see on her furrowed face
A smile crack right across
Like splitting wood, her scaly hand
Make a genuine sign of the cross.

Rimbaud: Democracy

The colours on parade, dipping past the filthy bricks of this garrison town. Boots, newly issued, stutter on the cobbles: but we can keep step.

We'll be posted overseas, to the big Base Depots. White buildings in long straight lines, like the Big City itself, but with everything laid on, just for us. It'll be the biggest, best-run brothel in the world. If the students riot, it'll be us reservists who're called out.

East of Suez or thereabouts — where the cold beer is grateful to the clay that gurgles it up, and the temper rises nicely after meals. We'll make the black bastards work: leader-writers will talk about the Commonwealth.

Anywhere, to get away from home. Glad to be back in the army, we'll use our loaves, all right. We can't pass exams, but we get our feet under the table. Everyone else can get fucked. Progress we call it.

By – The – Right – Quick – MARCH

Instruction for my Godson
(To William Redgrove)

God help me, I'm supposed to see you're told
All about God the Father. So my beard mutters:
There are always two fathers, one Good and one
    Bad.
You can't miss the Bad One, he's always around,
Particularly first thing in the morning,
Scruffy and screaming for a razor-blade,
Wondering who to eat up for his breakfast –
He won't eat you however much he shouts.
I'm not trying to sell you bad old Nobadaddy –
Learn to shrug off his sessions on his throne
Farting thunderbolts and belching clouds.

The Good One has a different way with clouds; he
    watches.
He knows fifty-seven ways at least of looking at
    them,
He addresses them politely, and his looking
Can hold them still in the sky.

Letter to Ken Russell

Dear Russ, you're dead and dust. I didn't know.
I've heard it only at removes. For X,
Who we detested, passed it on from Y,
For whom we had a jeering kind of fondness –
He read about it in the Old School Journal –
One way of keeping up.

'Organic disease' were the words. Which one?
Which painful monster had you when you died?
As good a life as me, I would have said –
You're one-up now, you smug old bastard:
'Christ, boy,' you say, 'I'm dead now.'
Stop dribbling bubbles of laughter round your
     pipe.

How many years since both of us owed letters?
Let's offer the usual excuses –
Marriage, of course, wives don't get on,
The housing-shortage, railway fares, etc.,
Weak putting-off, sheer bloody laziness.
We didn't want to say the way things went
Pissed on the hopes we entertained,
Naïve, of course, but vivid and still pissed on –
The old gang born again in young careerists –
(Christ, boy, they're reading *The Times* now!)
As if we hadn't known all this before!

Gratitude, now, is what's appropriate.
How glad I am I've had your company!
After an adolescent's silly days
Of idle mornings, hypochondriac afternoons,

Thick skies that frowned and trees that swayed
    foreboding,
What evenings of relief have set me free!
Evenings of beer and talk, bezique, Tchaikovsky,
Hysterical evenings screeching at dull flicks,
And evenings when we gossiped into movement
The huge grotesques we knew, to keep us sane –
Hadji, Wokko, Nodger hardly knew themselves
And should we meet would start us off again.
'Christ, boy,' you say, 'Listen to this.'
Something new, I expect, about Taverner's
    sponges,
Drying, between the lying maps, in rows.
The sods today are duller and more utter,
But deadlier, deadlier still.

A formal ending I can't manage.
We've been solemn enough before, at Party
    meetings,
Constructive, eager, serious, ineffective ...
'Yours fraternally,' then. And grin your inverted
    commas.
Help me to tell the truth and not feel dull.

CHARLES CAUSLEY

A Ballad for Katharine of Aragon

Queen of England, 1509-33
Buried in Peterborough Cathedral

As I walked down by the river
Down by the frozen fen
I saw the grey cathedral
With the eyes of a child of ten.
O the railway arch is smoky
As the Flying Scot goes by
And but for the Education Act
Go Jumper Cross and I.

But war is a bitter bugle
That all must learn to blow
And it didn't take long to stop the song
In the dirty Italian snow.
O war is a casual mistress
And the world is her double bed
She has a few charms in her mechanized arms
But you wake up and find yourself dead.

The olive tree in winter
Casts her banner down
And the priest in white and scarlet
Comes up from the muddy town.
O never more will Jumper
Watch the Flying Scot go by
His funeral knell was a six-inch shell
Singing across the sky.

The Queen of Castile has a daughter
Who won't come home again
She lies in the grey cathedral

Under the arms of Spain.
O the Queen of Castile has a daughter
Torn out by the roots
Her lovely breast in a cold stone chest
Under the farmers' boots.

Now I like a Spanish party
And many O many the day
I have watched them swim as the night came dim
In Algeciras Bay.
O the high sierra was thunder
And the seven-branched river of Spain
Came down to the sea to plunder
The heart of the sailor again.

O shall I leap in the river
And knock upon paradise door
For a gunner of twenty-seven and a half
And a queen of twenty-four?
From the almond tree by the river
I watch the sky with a groan
For Jumper and Kate are always out late
And I lie here alone.

Nursery Rhyme of Innocence and Experience

I had a silver penny
  And an apricot tree
And I said to the sailor
  On the white quay

'Sailor O sailor
  Will you bring me
If I give you my penny
  And my apricot tree

'A fez from Algeria
  An Arab drum to beat
A little gilt sword
  And a parakeet?'

And he smiled and he kissed me
  As strong as death
And I saw his red tongue
  And I felt his sweet breath

'You may keep your penny
  And your apricot tree
And I'll bring your presents
  Back from sea.'

O the ship dipped down
  On the rim of the sky
And I waited while three
  Long summers went by

Then one steel morning
  On the white quay
I saw a grey ship
  Come in from sea

Slowly she came
  Across the bay
For her flashing rigging
  Was shot away

All round her wake
  The seabirds cried
And flew in and out
  Of the hole in her side

Slowly she came
  In the path of the sun
And I heard the sound
  Of a distant gun

And a stranger came running
  Up to me
From the deck of the ship
  And he said, said he

'*O are you the boy*
  Who would wait on the quay
With the silver penny
  And the apricot tree?

'*I've a plum-coloured fez*
  And a drum for thee
And a sword and a parakeet
  From over the sea.'

'O where is the sailor
  With bold red hair?
And what is that volley
  On the bright air?

'O where are the other
    Girls and boys?
And why have you brought me
    Children's toys?'

Demobilization Leave

I have seen the white tiger,
Imagination,
In the Douanier Rousseau forest:
Isosceles leaves and a waterfall of compasses.
And although I am writing in Cornwall, in winter,
And the rain is coming in from the moor,
Trincomali, ah, Trincomali!
The Technicolor market, the monkeys and chickens,
The painted boats at Vegetable Jetty,
The rattling lizard and the bored crow
In the burning graveyard:

Here lies David Kelly, Naval Stores Officer,
Died of the Fever,
1816.

O the drums and the pythons and the trick of the mango
        tree,
The warrior Buddha with the brandished sword,
The rosewood elephants and the porcupine cigarette
        boxes.
O the fire opal, zircon and water sapphire,
And the warm beer and peanuts in the P.O.'s canteen.
The Chinese cafés, and the rickshaw-boys
Grinning and gambling by the fishmarket.
The rings from Kandy and the black ivory elephants
Crossing the eternal bridge for the mantelshelves
Of thousands and thousands of sailors.
And the carrier and her exhausted planes
Lying in the oily harbour,
Hands to bathe
And the liberty-boats

Buzzing over the water.
O the sickly lime-juice at Elephant House
And the cooking that looks of the West
But tastes, O tastes of the East.

And they say,
'You must be fed up with your leave,
Fifty-six days is a long time,
You'll start work before it's over –
You'll be tired of nothing to do,
Nothing to think of,
Nothing to write about.
Yes, you'll go back to the office
Soon.'

At the Grave of John Clare

Walking in the scythed churchyard, around the locked
  church,
Walking among the oaks and snails and mossed
  inscriptions
At first we failed to find the grave.
But a girl said: 'There he is: there is John Clare.'
And we stood, silent, by the ridged stone,
A stone of grey cheese.
There were no flowers for the dead ploughman
As the gilt clock fired off the hour,
Only the words:
A poet is born not made.

The dove-grey village lay in the Dutch landscape:
The level-crossing and the fields of wet barley,
The almshouses, the school, the Ebenezer Chapel,
The two pubs, and the signposts
To Stamford, To Maxey
From the pages of biography.
And later, sitting in the church
Among the unstuffed hassocks,
And smoking a pipe on the gate
At Maxey Crossing,
I thought of the dead poet:

Of the books and letters in the Peterborough Museum,
The huge, mad writing.
Of the way he walked, with one foot in the furrow,
Or hurried, terrified, as a child to fetch the milk from
  Maxey
Expecting from every turn a Caliban.
Of London, Charles Lamb and Hazlitt,

The bad grammar, the spelling, the invented words,
And the poetry bursting like a diamond bomb.
I thought of the last days, the old man
Sitting alone in the porch of All Saints' in Northampton,
And the dead poet trundling home to Helpston.

O Clare! Your poetry clear, translucent
As your lovely name,
I salute you with tears.
And, coming out on the green from *The Parting Pot,*
I notice a bicycle-tyre
Hanging from the high stone feathers of your
     monument.

King's College Chapel

When to the music of Byrd or Tallis,
   The ruffed boys singing in the blackened stalls,
The candles lighting the small bones on their faces,
   The Tudors stiff in marble on the walls,

There comes to evensong Elizabeth or Henry,
   Rich with brocade, pearl, golden lilies, at the altar,
The scarlet lions leaping on their bosoms,
   Pale royal hands fingering the crackling psalter,

Henry is thinking of his lute and of backgammon,
   Elizabeth follows the waving song, the mystery,
Proud in her red wig and green jewelled favours;
   They sit in their white lawn sleeves, as cool as history.

Able Seaman Hodge Remembers Ceylon

O the blackthorn and the wild cherry
   And the owl in the rotting oak tree
Are part of the Cornish landscape
   Which is more than can be said for me.

O the drum and the coconut fiddle
   And the taste of Arabian tea
The Vimto on the veranda
   And the arrack shops on the quay.

I wish I'd never heard of Kandy
   Or the song in the whiteflower tree.
*(There's a thousand loafing matelots in the old
    base ship*
   An' I wish that one of them was me)

O the pineapple salads of Colombo
   The wine-bar at Trincomali
My bonnie lies over the ocean:
   The brilliant Arabian Sea.

The Seasons in North Cornwall

O spring has set off her green fuses
    Down by the Tamar today,
And careless, like tidemarks, the hedges
    Are bursting with almond and may.

Here lie I, waiting for old summer,
    A red face and straw-coloured hair has he:
I shall meet him on the road from Marazion
    And the Mediterranean Sea.

September has flung a spray of rooks
    On the sea-chart of the sky,
The tall shipmasts crack in the forest
    And the banners of autumn fly.

My room is a bright glass cabin,
    All Cornwall thunders at my door,
And the white ships of winter lie
    In the sea-roads of the moor.

The Life of the Poet

Lock the door, Schoolmaster,
    Keep the children in.
The river in spate at the schoolyard gate
    Roars like original sin.

Watch your thermometer, Sister,
    The patient refuses to die.
The dizzy germ and the raving sperm
    Can't keep his powder dry.

Strike the drum, Bandmaster,
    Under the rig of the moon.
The girls come whirling, their veils unfurling,
    But what has become of the tune?

Answer the door, Squire,
    Your manners are on the table.
There's a job to be done with a humane gun
    If the horse is still in the stable.

Draw your revolver, Banker,
    Shoot him down like a dole.
You may gird his loins with nickel coins
    But where's his immortal soul?

Open the book, Parson,
    See whom you will save.
They say you're as kind as an open mind
    Or an open grave.

Fall out, fall out, Gabriel,
    You might as well hit the hay.
Your visitor wears the spinning airs
    And won't be round today.

To a Poet Who Has Never Travelled

As I rose like a lover from the ravished sea
My cold mouth stuffed with jewels and with sand,
The fire falling at my hair and hand,
(Her mother the moon waiting for the fee)
I saw you lying by the listening tree.

The infant pain lay sleeping at your side
Rocked by the naked fingers of the tide,
But you saw not my shaking ship, nor me.

I spread my sweating sea-charts at your knee
My rooted tongue burgeoning apes and roses
As noon the sally-port of morning closes,
My crew hallooing at the drunken quay.

My bonny barque was sundered at your door!
You smiled, for you had seen it all before.

Shore Leave

See the moon her yellow landau
Draws across the fainting sky.
The white owl round my window wanders
As I hurry by.

Night the Negro lays his fingers
On the lily-breast of day.
Sleep beckons like a gentle lover
But I hasten away.

On the sea the ships are leaping
To the islands of the sun.
On the deck the sailors sleeping
Would I were one!

In my ear no more the music
Of the tree the summer long,
Only the unfaithful ocean
And the Sirens' song.

I Am the Great Sun

(From a Normandy crucifix of 1632)

I am the great sun, but you do not see me,
    I am your husband, but you turn away.
I am the captive, but you do not free me,
    I am the captain you will not obey.

I am the truth, but you will not believe me,
    I am the city where you will not stay,
I am your wife, your child, but you will leave me,
    I am that God to whom you will not pray.

I am your counsel, but you do not hear me,
    I am the lover whom you will betray,
I am the victor, but you do not cheer me,
    I am the holy dove whom you will slay.

    I am your life, but if you will not name me,
    Seal up your soul with tears, and never blame me.

Timothy Winters

Timothy Winters comes to school
With eyes as wide as a football-pool,
Ears like bombs and teeth like splinters:
A blitz of a boy is Timothy Winters.

His belly is white, his neck is dark,
And his hair is an exclamation-mark.
His clothes are enough to scare a crow
And through his britches the blue winds blow.

When teacher talks he won't hear a word
And he shoots down dead the arithmetic-bird,
He licks the patterns off his plate
And he's not even heard of the Welfare State.

Timothy Winters has bloody feet
And he lives in a house on Suez Street,
He sleeps in a sack on the kitchen floor
And they say there aren't boys like him any more.

Old Man Winters likes his beer
And his missus ran off with a bombardier,
Grandma sits in the grate with a gin
And Timothy's dosed with an aspirin.

The Welfare Worker lies awake
But the law's as tricky as a ten-foot snake,
So Timothy Winters drinks his cup
And slowly goes on growing up.

At Morning Prayers the Master helves
For children less fortunate than ourselves,
And the loudest response in the room is when
Timothy Winters roars 'Amen!'

So come one angel, come on ten:
Timothy Winters says 'Amen
Amen amen amen amen.'
Timothy Winters, Lord.
                    Amen.

Hawthorn White

Hawthorn white, hawthorn red
Hanging in the garden at my head
Tell me simple, tell me true
When comes the winter what must I do?

I have a house with chimneys four
I have a silver bell on the door,
A single hearth and a single bed.
  Not enough, the hawthorn said.

I have a lute, I have a lyre
I have a yellow cat by my fire,
A nightingale to my tree is tied.
  That bird looks sick, the hawthorn sighed.

I write on paper pure as milk
I lie on sheets of Shantung silk,
On my green breast no sin has snowed.
  You'll catch your death, the hawthorn crowed.

My purse is packed with a five-pound note
The watchdogs in my garden gloat.
I blow the bagpipe down my side.
  Better blow your safe, the hawthorn cried.

My pulse is steady as my clock
My wits are wise as the weathercock.
Twice a year we are overhauled.
  It's Double Summer-Time! the hawthorn called.

I have a horse with wings for feet
I have chicken each day to eat.

When I was born the church-bells rang.
  Only one at a time, the hawthorn sang.

I have a cellar, I have a spread
The bronze blood runs round my bulkhead:
Why is my heart as light as lead?
  Love is not there, the hawthorn said.

The Prisoners of Love

Trapped in their tower, the prisoners of love
Loose their last message on the failing air.
The troops of Tyre assault with fire the grove
Where Venus veils with light her lovely hair.

Trembles the tide beneath the tall martello
That decks the harbour with its wreck of thunder,
Fretting with flowers white and flowers yellow
The fosse of flame into its last surrender.

Night, on my truckle-bed your ease of slumber
Sleep in salt arms the steering night away.
Abandoned in the fireship moon, one ember
Glows with the rose that is the distant day.

The prisoners rise and rinse their skies of stone,
But in their jailers' eyes they meet their own.

Betjeman, 1984

I saw him in the Airstrip Gardens
    (Fahrenheit at 45 1)
Feeding automative orchids
    With a little plastic bun,
While above his brickwork cranium
    Burned the trapped and troubled sun.

'Where is Piper? Where is Pontefract?
    (Devil take my boiling pate!)
Where is Pam? And where's Myfanwy?
    Don't remind me of the date!
Can it be that I am *really*
    Knocking on for 78?

'In my splendid State Apartment
    Underneath a secret lock
Finger now forbidden treasures
    (Pray for me St Enodoc!):
TV plate and concrete lamp-post
    And a single nylon sock.

'Take your ease, pale-haired admirer,
    As I, half the century saner,
Pour a vintage Mazawattee
    Through the Marks and Spencer strainer
In a *genuine* British Railways
    (Luton Made) cardboard container.

'Though they say my verse-compulsion
    Lacks an interstellar drive,
Reading Beverley and Daphne

Keeps *my* sense of words alive.
Lord, but *how* much beauty was there
Back in 1955!'

Time Like a Saucy Trooper

Time like a saucy trooper took my true-love
    In the stiff corn that stands above the bay,
Never a backward glance he gave his new love,
    But whistled a tune and slowly rode away.

About her brow my love winds the white hours
    And binds her breast with sprigs of rosemary,
Through her thin hands she threads the winter flowers
    And lies with eyes as pale as the snowy sea.

Ruined the roses on the giddy river
    That heaps its tears upon the sleeping narrows,
The archer sun unships his candid quiver
    And tips with azure all his blazing arrows.

Now the swift seasons, coasting shores of sorrow,
    On the wild waters sink their chinking floes,
And for the tender promise of tomorrow
    They leave the lily, but uproot the rose.

I made my love a hive of yellow honey,
    I laid my love a cabin on the water,
Two beds I bought of my new-minted money
    For my true-love and me, and for her daughter.

Never across the water comes she winging,
    Bright is our bed as on its boughten day,
And all the night I hear my lover singing
    The song the soldier sang as he rode away.

Ballad of the Five Continents

In blue Bristol city at tall-tide I wandered
   Down where the sea-masts their signals were shining,
   I heard a proud seaman on the poop-deck reclining
Shout to the stars that about the ship blundered
   On the high harbour lie six shifty daughters
   Their bodies are straight, their eyes are wide
   Here is the key of their burly bedchamber
I have unlocked it, I replied.

As I went down Water Street beneath the blond sun
   The trees of cold Christmas screaming with starlings
   Sweet screamed the birds as my delicate darlings
Scanned at my hand the black-butted gun
   Think of the collar my bonny, my beauty
   Think of the hangman with hands so red
   Pray, pray that he does his duty
I am that hangman, I said.

As I walked in Wine Street the silk snow was falling
   And night in her Asian hair hung her comb,
   Soft sang the yellow-faced seaman of home
The gong and the coconut-fiddle recalling
   In the vermilion forest the dancer
   Adorns with gold thorns his holy head
   Will you not seize his hands, his fingers?
I am the dance, I said.

In Bread Street in summer we saw the boys hauling
   The Yankee-white wheat on the bowl of the bay,
   Between us the sword of the sun where we lay
Bloody with poppies, the warm sky our shawling
   Sly sing the sirens on the coast of California

The oyster-fingered, the easy-eyed,
Tiding their tune in the gin-wicked palaces
The song is mine, I cried.

Down by the dockside the green ships groaning
Ten-roped writhe on the ragged sea,
Blesséd are they with the laurel tree
Now in the prow stands a saint for the stoning
Sound the salt bell on the mound of the ocean
Fish for a prayer in the pool of the dead
When the storm strikes, speak the word on the waters
I am that word, I said.

ENVOI

I am the Prince
I am the lowly
I am the damned
I am the holy.
My hands are ten knives.
I am the dove
Whose wings are murder.
My name is love.

Innocent's Song

Who's that knocking on the window,
Who's that standing at the door,
What are all those presents
Lying on the kitchen floor?

Who is the smiling stranger
With hair as white as gin,
What is he doing with the children
And who could have let him in?

Why has he rubies on his fingers,
A cold, cold crown on his head,
Why, when he caws his carol,
Does the salty snow run red?

Why does he ferry my fireside
As a spider on a thread,
His fingers made of fuses
And his tongue of gingerbread?

Why does the world before him
Melt in a million suns,
Why do his yellow, yearning eyes
Burn like saffron buns?

Watch where he comes walking
Out of the Christmas flame,
Dancing, double-talking:

Herod is his name.

Mother, Get Up, Unbar the Door

Mother, get up, unbar the door,
Throw wide the window-pane,
I see a man stand all covered in sand
Outside in Vicarage Lane.

His body is shot with seventy stars,
His face is cold as Cain,
His coat is a crust of desert dust
And he comes from Alamein.

He has not felt the flaking frost,
He has not felt the rain,
And not one blow of the burning snow
Since the night that he was slain.

O mother, in your husband's arms
Too long now you have lain,
Rise up, my dear, your true-love's here
Upon the peaceful plain.

Though, mother, on your broken brow
Forty long years are lain,
The soldier they slew at twenty-two
Never a one does gain.

I will unlock the fine front-door
And snap the silver chain,
And meek as milk in my skin of silk
I'll ease him of his pain.

My breast has been for years eighteen
As white as Charles's wain,
But now I'm had by a soldier lad
Whistling *Lili Marlene*.

Farewell to Jack, farewell to Jim,
And farewell Mary Jane,
Farewell the good green sisterhood
Knitting at purl and plain.

Go wash the water from your eye,
The bullet from your brain.
I'm drowned as a dove in the tunnel of love
And I'll never come home again.

Healing a Lunatic Boy

Trees turned and talked to me,
Tigers sang,
Houses put on leaves,
Water rang.
Flew in, flew out
On my tongue's thread
A speech of birds
From my hurt head.

At my fine loin
Fire and cloud kissed,
Rummaged the green bone
Beneath my wrist.
I saw a sentence
Of fern and tare
Write with loud light
The mineral air.

On a stopped morning
The city spoke,
In my rich mouth
Oceans broke.
No more on the spun shore
I walked unfed.
I drank the sweet sea,
Stones were bread.

Then came the healer
Grave as grass,
His hair of water
And hands of glass.
I watched at his tongue

The white words eat,
In death, dismounted
At his stabbed feet.

Now river is river
And tree is tree,
My house stands still
As the northern sea.
On my hundred of parables
I heard him pray,
Seize my smashed world,
Wrap it away.

Now the pebble is sour,
The birds beat high,
The fern is silent,
The river dry.
A seething summer
Burned to bone
Feeds at my mouth
But finds a stone.

For an Ex Far East Prisoner of War

I am that man with helmet made of thorn
Who wandered naked in the desert place,
Wept, with the sweating sky, that I was born
And wore disaster in my winter face.

I am that man who asked no hate, nor pity.
I am that man, five-wounded, on the tree.
I am that man, walking his native city,
Hears his dead comrade cry, *Remember me!*

I am that man whose brow with blood was wet,
Returned, as Lazarus, from the dead to live.
I am that man, long-counselled to forget,
Facing a fearful victory, to forgive:

And seizing these two words, with the sharp sun
Beat them, like sword and ploughshare, into one.

My Friend Maloney

My friend Maloney, eighteen,
   Swears like a sentry,
Got into trouble two years back
   With the local gentry.

Parson and squire's sons
   Informed a copper.
The magistrate took one look at Maloney.
   Fixed him proper.

Talked of the crime of youth,
   The innocent victim.
Maloney never said a blind word
   To contradict him.

Maloney of Gun Street,
   Back of the Nuclear Mission,
Son of the town whore,
   Blamed television.

Justice, as usual, triumphed.
   Everyone felt fine.
Things went deader.
   Maloney went up the line.

Maloney learned one lesson:
   Never play the fool
With the products of especially a minor
   Public school.

Maloney lost a thing or two
   At that institution.

First shirt, second innocence,
   The old irresolution.

Found himself a girl-friend,
　Sharp suit, sharp collars.
Maloney on a moped,
　Pants full of dollars.

College boys on the corner
　In striped, strait blazers
Look at old Maloney,
　Eyes like razors.

You don't need talent, says Maloney.
　You don't need looks.
All I got you got, fellers.
　You can keep your thick books.

Parson got religion,
　Squire, in the end, the same.
The magistrate went over the wall.
　Life, said Maloney, 's a game.

Consider then the case of Maloney,
　College boys, parson, squire, beak.
Who was the victor and who was the victim?
　Speak.

Three Masts

Three masts has the thrusting ship,
Three masts will she wear
When she like Christ our Saviour
Walks on the watery stair.

One stands at the fore
To meet the weather wild
As He who once in winter
Was a little child.

One grows after
From step to the sky
For He who once was keel-hauled
And hung up to die.

One stands amidships
Between fore and mizzen
Pointing to paradise
For He who is risen.

Three masts will grow on the green ship
Before she quits the quay,
For Father, Son, and Holy Ghost:
Blessed Trinity.

Johnny Alleluia

Johnny Alleluia
  In a seven-year cell
Watched the walking morning
  Didn't feel well,
Stretched for a string
  Of the leaping light,
Nailed it to his neck-bone
  Tacked it tight.

Up went Johnny
  In the blue, bold air,
You should have seen
  The screws all stare.
Johnny? they said,
  More lives than a cat.
Never should have thought he'd done
  A thing like that.

Johnny was a tinker,
  Tramped to the fair,
His kettles as bright
  As his tinplate hair.
With his tongue of chicken
  And his breast of ham
Johnny didn't give
  A tinker's damn.

It was Good old Johnny,
  And Johnny here's the key,
And Johnny put your hand
  Where it shouldn't be.
O the girls all laughed

And the boys didn't care
When Johnny came up
  Their kitchen stair.

But what is this blade
  And what is this stone,
And why don't you take
  A wife of your own?
Why do you wear
  Your breeches so tight,
And what is this drum
  Of dynamite?

I sharpen my knife
  On the winding stone
To cut me an apple
  From the branch of bone.
My pants so tight
  Keep my legs apart,
And I blast with powder
  The human heart.

Is this a bunch
  Of skeleton keys,
And what is this wax
  Under your chemise?
Why are your eyes
  So clear, my son,
And you still under
  Twenty-one?

Under my shirt
  My keys and my wax
Unlock the body

And silence the cracks.
I hear in my heart
   The gold blood gad
As it did in the days
   When Adam was a lad.

It was Now then, Johnny,
   And Johnny take care,
For boys like you
   There's nothing to spare.
In the lake of love
   You're sure to drown,
You can't walk on water
   In this town.

You must keep your fingers
   To yourself
And your lollipop eye
   From another man's shelf.
And Johnny don't take
   Too long a pull
At all things bright
   And beautiful.

They shanghai'd Johnny
   In a squinting cell
With modern plumbing
   And a view of hell.
They disinfected
   His public parts
And sketched his soul
   On little charts.

So he cast off shore
   And swung to sea.

The Governor wept,
　　He said, said he,
It was ever thus!
　　And shook his head.

I'm damned if it was,
　　Young Johnny said.

Grave by the Sea

By the crunching, Cornish sea
Walk the man and walk the lover,
Innocent as fish that fare
In the high and hooking air,
And their deaths discover.

Beneath, you said, this turning tree,
With granite eye and stare of sand,
His heart as candid as the clay,
A seaman from the stropping bay
Took to the land.

Once this calmed, crystal hand was free
And rang the changes of the heart:
Love, like his life, a world wherein
The white-worm sin wandered not in.
Death played no part.

Wreathed, and with ringing fingers he
Passed like a prince upon the day
And from its four and twenty towers
Shot with his shaft the haggard hours,
Hauled them away.

So he set from the shaken quay
His foot upon the ocean floor
And from the wanting water's teeth
The ice-faced gods above, beneath,
Spat him ashore.

Now, in the speaking of the sea,
He waits under this written stone,

And kneeling at his freezing frame
I scrub my eye to see his name

And read my own.

Index of First Lines

INDEX